Raising Pilot

by **Marcie Aboff**

Illustrated by **Pam Tanzey**

CELEBRATION PRESS

Pearson Learning Group

Contents

Chapter 1

A New Family Member

As soon as Hayley Douglas came home from school, her big collie dog, Koko, bounded up to her, barking and wagging his tail. Hayley bent down and gave Koko a big hug, and he licked her face. When she walked into the kitchen, Koko followed her closely.

Hayley's father came out of his office. He was a writer for a magazine, and he worked at home most days.

"Hi, Hayley," he said, "how was school?"

"It was okay," Hayley said. She dropped her backpack on the kitchen table and went to get an apple from a bowl. "I have a math worksheet to complete. What's for dinner?"

"I'm going to put a chicken in the oven pretty soon," her father answered. "That reminds me—we're going to have a quick family meeting at dinnertime."

"Why, what's wrong?" asked Hayley. Her family always had their meetings during relaxed Sunday dinners, not busy Wednesday nights.

Her father laughed. "Don't worry, Hayley. This is *good* news, not bad news."

Hayley's heart jumped. "Tell me now, tell me now!" she begged.

"No, not yet," her father said.

"Does Mom know?" asked Hayley.

"Yes, Mom knows," Hayley's father said. "Eat your apple, do your homework, and we'll talk about it when she comes home."

Hayley heard the door slam, and Koko barked again. Hayley's older brother, Seth, hurried into the kitchen.

"We're going to have a family meeting," Hayley informed her brother.

"No time for that," Seth said as he grabbed an apple. "I have to change my clothes for soccer practice."

"We're not meeting till dinnertime," Hayley said, "and dad said it's about something good. Any idea what it is?"

"Maybe we won the lottery," Seth called as he ran upstairs to his bedroom.

When Hayley's mom came home from work, and Seth had returned from soccer practice, the Douglas family sat down at the dinner table. "So what's going on?" Hayley asked.

"Well," her father said, "your mom and I have been thinking about getting another dog, a special kind of dog."

Hayley loved animals and had already decided to be a veterinarian when she grew up. "Another dog would be great!" she declared, grinning.

"Another dog, like loco Koko?" Seth asked. He looked at Koko, who was sitting next to Hayley. Hayley frowned, because she didn't like Seth's nickname for Koko. Koko wasn't loco, or crazy—he was the best dog in the entire universe.

"This would be a *very* special puppy," Hayley's mom explained. "We would actually be raising a guide-dog puppy."

"You mean we'd be taking care of a dog that helps blind people?" asked Hayley.

"Yes," her father said, "a dog like the one that helps Aunt Lily." Aunt Lily was Hayley's great-aunt. A few years before, she had developed an eye disease that made her lose her eyesight. With her guide dog, Aunt Lily could walk places, shop, and ride on the bus.

"Hayley, tell Koko to stop begging at the table!" her dad added, and everyone laughed.

"What we would do," her mom said, "is train the puppy and help it become accustomed to new people and places. We'd take it to puppy training classes, too. When it's between 14 and 18 months old, it would go back to the guide-dog school for formal training. Several months later, the dog would be given to a visually impaired person to help the person live independently."

That sounds great! Hayley thought. She wanted to help to raise the guide dog.

"Because I'm home most of the day," her father said, "I will be the main puppy raiser. However, this is a family project. Tomorrow night, a training leader from the guide-dog school will come to our home and tell us about the program. Then, we'll decide if we would like to raise the puppy."

"I'll help you!" said Hayley. "I can walk the dog sometimes, and I'll help it to make friends with Koko."

"Dad, Koko won't be jealous of another dog in the house, will he?" Seth wanted to know.

"I don't think so, Seth. Koko always behaves well around other dogs, and it's good for guide dogs to be exposed to other pets."

"How old will the puppy be?" asked Hayley.

"The puppy will be at least eight weeks old," Mom said, smiling. "Any more questions?"

Hayley shook her head.

The next evening, the training leader, Christine Parker, interviewed Hayley's family. She talked to all of them, then asked to do a check of the home and yard for safety measures. Hayley proudly showed her room to Christine.

"I think you'll make excellent puppy raisers," Christine said. "I will bring your dog in two weeks." Hayley could hardly wait.

Chapter 2

Hello, Pilot!

When she heard the doorbell ring, Hayley raced to open the door.

"Here he is, everyone!" Christine said, smiling as she held up a dog carrier. "His name is Pilot." The curled-up little puppy had light yellow fur, a black nose, and big black eyes.

"He's a Labrador retriever," Christine explained. Hayley's family crowded around Christine as she took Pilot out of the carrier, then handed him to Mr. Douglas.

"Can I hold him next?" Hayley begged, petting the Labrador puppy. She was thrilled when her father placed the dog in her arms. Next to Koko, he looked like a toy dog.

"Try putting him down," Christine suggested, so Hayley gently put Pilot down on the floor. Koko bounded over to Pilot and barked. The puppy was so scared that he ran and hid behind the couch. He peered out cautiously.

"Koko, be quiet!" Seth said with a serious tone of voice. "You're frightening Pilot."

"It might take a little time for Koko and Pilot to grow comfortable with each other," Christine said. Mrs. Douglas bent over the couch and gently lifted Pilot, placing him on a cozy blanket in a big wire crate.

"You'll be safe in here while Koko gets used to you," Hayley's mom said to the puppy.

Christine opened a big orange bag. "I have lots of things to leave with you for Pilot," she said.

She handed Mr. Douglas a puppy-training manual and a pack to wear around his waist. "You can keep puppy treats for Pilot in the pack when you go out," she said. "If you go to a store, you need to ask the manager if Seeing Eye puppies are allowed. The law says that Seeing Eye *dogs* have to be allowed inside, but it doesn't say anything about accommodating Seeing Eye *puppies*."

Then Christine took out ID tags and a small green jacket that said GUIDE DOG PUPPY. "Pilot should wear an ID tag and the green jacket whenever he goes out in public. They let people know he is being trained to live with a blind person."

Hayley didn't like Christine's last words. She didn't want to think about giving Pilot up someday. *That won't happen for a long time*, she told herself.

"Mr. Douglas, I know you said you'll be the main puppy raiser," Christine said, "so I will see you at the training class next Saturday."

Hayley quickly looked up at her father. "Dad, I want to raise Pilot, too!" she declared. "Can I be your assistant and go to the class with you?"

Hayley's dad smiled. "You may do that if Christine says you can," he answered.

"That would be great, Hayley," Christine said. "For now, just give Pilot plenty of love and let him get used to your home. In fact, I think Koko has calmed down, so why don't you hold Pilot again now?"

When Hayley took Pilot out of his crate and held him on her lap, Koko jumped up next to them and wagged his tail. "Koko, I know you want to play," Hayley said, "but just give Pilot some time to get used to us."

Christine smiled and said, "I'll see you both at the training class next week."

Chapter 3

Training Class

The following week, Hayley and her dad drove to the training center with Pilot. There were many people there, mostly adults.

Christine welcomed Hayley and her dad. "Did you bring Pilot's green jacket? Good— please put it on him," she told them.

Some of the puppies were being introduced to the program, as Pilot was. Other puppies had been in training for several months.

When all the puppies and their trainers sat in a circle, Hayley noticed two other young people. One was a teenage girl, and the other was a boy who looked a little older than Hayley.

Christine talked about something important that the group needed to understand. "Never give your puppy table scraps or let the dog eat food that he's found on the ground," she said.

We give Koko table scraps all the time, Hayley thought. She knew she had a lot to learn about raising a guide puppy.

"This would be important," Christine explained, "if a blind person was walking down the street and his or her guide dog saw some food on the sidewalk. The dog would need to know not to stop and eat the food. Guide dogs must know their jobs are to help their owners," she said firmly.

Next, Christine talked about getting the puppies used to different noises. "Our dogs need to be exposed to various sounds, so they get used to all the different places their owners might go," she said. "The dogs learn not to be distracted by applause at concerts or by the racket of city streets."

Christine had everyone clap loudly. Some of the younger puppies barked, including Pilot. Many of the older puppies raised their ears alertly, but they did not bark.

"Wonderful!" said Christine. "You can really see the progress in the older dogs. The younger puppies will learn soon, too."

After the class, Hayley and her father went
outside with Pilot. The boy who looked a little
older than Hayley came up to her.

"Your puppy is cute," the boy said.

"Thanks," Hayley said. "Your dog is cute,
too." She looked at the black Labrador retriever
on the boy's leash. It was almost as big as Koko.

"How old is your dog?" she asked.

"Stacie is exactly one year old," he said.

The boy said his name was Daniel. "I'm the main raiser in the family," he told Hayley. "My mom helps me, but I do most of the training."

"Wow! How old are you?" Hayley asked. Daniel explained that he was twelve.

"You're so lucky," Hayley told Daniel. "I'm helping my father to raise Pilot, but Dad is the main trainer."

Daniel smiled. "I've got to get to a practice, so I'll see you at the next class," he said.

On the way home, Hayley chattered nonstop to her father. She couldn't wait to tell her mother and Seth about everything they had learned about raising Pilot properly.

Pilot had become used to his carrier. He slept peacefully inside, his sweet face resting between his front paws.

Chapter 4

Pilot Goes to the Mall

In the weeks that followed, Pilot settled in comfortably with the Douglas family's routine. Hayley's father walked Pilot every day and took him to the veterinarian for his shots. Hayley loved helping her dad train Pilot and going with him to the puppy training classes.

Pilot played with Koko now, and the two dogs ran around the enclosed backyard. Sometimes, though, Koko got too boisterous and Pilot would run away.

Hayley would put Pilot in his crate then, but Koko sat right next to the crate. Whenever Pilot moved, Koko stood up and pressed his wet nose against the crate.

When Pilot was a little over three months old, Hayley and her family started taking him out in public. Pilot loved car rides and seemed to enjoy the trips. Seth needed new basketball shoes, so they decided to take Pilot to the mall.

Hayley was sorry to leave Koko behind, but she knew Koko wouldn't be allowed in the mall. She knelt down and stroked his fur.

"Don't be lonely, Koko. When I come back, I will have a surprise for you." She planned to stop at a pet store in the mall to get Koko a new squeaky toy.

The streets were slippery with ice, and Hayley's dad drove cautiously. Inside the mall, people turned and smiled when they saw the puppy in the green jacket. Hayley felt very special.

A little girl with two pigtails ran up to Pilot. "Look at the puppy, Mommy!" she squealed. Then, she suddenly pulled Pilot's tail. The little girl's mother scolded her.

"I'm so sorry," the girl's mother apologized.

Mr. Douglas explained that Pilot was training to be a guide dog. He looked at the little girl. "It's important not to pet a dog you don't know," he told her gently. "You don't want to scare the dog or possibly get hurt." Mr. Douglas put Pilot in a sitting position, then he told the girl she could pet Pilot on the top of his head now.

Pilot sat still for a moment before jumping playfully at the girl. Hayley's father gave Pilot's leash a tug. "No!" he said firmly, correcting Pilot's behavior. When Pilot sat down again, he said "Good boy," and gave Pilot a puppy treat.

"Pilot wouldn't hurt you," Mr. Douglas told the girl, "but he needs to learn to sit still."

At a sneaker store, Hayley's father asked to speak with the store manager. After he explained that Pilot was a Seeing Eye puppy in training, the manager said it was all right for Pilot to be in the store.

Every time Seth tried on a pair of shoes, Pilot would take the laces between his teeth and pull. Seth laughed and patted Pilot.

Hayley and her mom decided to take Pilot to the pet store next. Hayley bought a big squeaky toy bone for Koko and another one for Pilot.

Later, at the food court, Pilot tried to get some food that was on the floor. "No!" said Hayley. "Sit, Pilot." It took a few tries, but at last Pilot sat and stayed.

When Hayley got home, she headed into the house to give Koko his new toy. Suddenly, she heard her father yell. Hayley turned around. Her father had slipped on the ice and had fallen to the ground! He held his foot in pain.

Chapter 5

Hayley Takes Charge

Hayley's mother took Mr. Douglas to the doctor. He had broken his ankle.

The doctor said that Mr. Douglas could sit at his computer, but he could not use the stairs. He would have to stay off his leg for six weeks! It was definitely time for a family meeting.

"Pilot and Koko must be walked every day," Hayley's mother said. "I don't want you to neglect your practices, Seth. Maybe I could try to get home from work half an hour earlier."

"*I* could be the main puppy raiser!" Hayley exclaimed. Her family looked at her in surprise.

Hayley found the training manual and showed it to her parents. "See—nine years is the minimum age, and I'm even older than that."

"It's a big responsibility," her father said. "You will have to come home directly after school to walk the dogs."

"I will!" Hayley promised eagerly.

"What about karate class?" her mom reminded her. Hayley had karate lessons every Tuesday after school, and she loved them.

"I forgot." Hayley's face fell. "Can you walk the dogs on Tuesdays, Mom?" she asked. "We won't have to give Pilot back, will we?"

"I don't have practices on Tuesdays. I'll make sure I'm home after school," Seth offered.

Hayley hugged her older brother. Her parents looked at each other and nodded. "You can be Pilot's main raiser now, Hayley," her father said. "We know you'll be very responsible."

Hayley read the entire training manual. She taught Pilot simple commands such as come, sit, stay, and heel. She included Koko, too, and before long, Koko's manners were improving along with Pilot's.

Hayley's mom dropped Hayley off at the training classes, and Hayley learned about the many skills Pilot would need to become a successful guide dog.

One day, Hayley walked with Pilot to a nearby card shop. "Didn't you see the sign? No dogs are allowed!" the clerk called loudly.

Hayley took a deep breath. "This is a guide dog puppy. May we stay in the store?"

"Sorry," the clerk apologized. "Of course the dog can stay inside." After that, Hayley felt more confident about taking Pilot places.

Mr. Douglas's ankle healed at last. He helped
Hayley to walk the dogs after school now.

In the spring, the family took Pilot to one of
Seth's baseball games. People kept coming up to
pet Pilot, and when Seth hit a home run,
everyone in the family missed it. "Hey, showoff!"
Seth teased Pilot afterward. "You're the main
attraction!"

Chapter 6

Pilot Grows Up

In the summer, Pilot learned how to swim in a lake. Pilot and Koko were great friends now. They played and jumped in the water together. When they fell asleep, Pilot nestled right by Koko's side.

Hayley loved Pilot so much that she wished the summer would never end—but of course, autumn came again. Pilot was now a mature, handsome dog.

One morning in November, Hayley's family got the telephone call they had been dreading. Christine Parker said that next month, Pilot would start his formal guide-dog training.

Hayley's heart sank at the news. She couldn't give up Pilot. She loved him exactly the same way she loved Koko. *I've spent so much time with Pilot. He's part of the family—I can't let him go now*, she thought.

Hayley's dad put his arm around Hayley. "We all love Pilot," he said, "but we knew the day would come when he would need to go for formal training. When Pilot passes training and testing, he'll be given to a blind person to help."

"What happens if Pilot doesn't pass his tests?" Hayley asked.

Her parents didn't say anything. Then her father quietly said, "If Pilot doesn't pass, then we might be able to keep him permanently."

Hayley's eyes opened wide. "Great!" she said. "I hope Pilot messes up."

"Oh, Hayley," her mother said. "You don't really mean that, do you?"

"I guess not," Hayley answered. Pilot was such a good dog—he deserved a chance to be a guide dog. She had known that one day she would have to let him go, but now that the time was here, all she could think of was how much she loved him.

Soon it was time for Christine to pick up Pilot. Hayley's parents and Seth all hugged him, and Hayley kissed him goodbye. Then she ran to her bedroom and cried.

That night, Koko began behaving strangely. He paced back and forth, looking lost, as if he were searching for his playmate. Koko even whined unhappily.

"I know how you feel," Hayley said, resting her head against Koko's furry body. "I miss Pilot, too."

Chapter 7

Graduation

Christine called several times during the four months that Pilot was in formal training. Every time she called, Hayley secretly hoped Christine would tell them that Pilot was misbehaving. However, Christine always told them how wonderfully Pilot was doing.

"You did a fantastic job raising Pilot," Christine told Hayley in April. "He passed all the tests with flying colors. Would you and your family like to attend Pilot's graduation?"

"Yes, absolutely!" Hayley exclaimed.

Hayley kept busy with her karate lessons and schoolwork. At last, Pilot's graduation day came.

Pilot barked when he saw Hayley's family, but he stayed by his new owner's side.

"Pilot helps me do so many things!" said his owner, whose name was Rosa. "Thank you for raising him. You all did a wonderful job."

Rosa's words made Hayley feel proud as she petted Pilot. Suddenly she had an idea. She decided to discuss it at the next family meeting.

A month later, the doorbell rang and Hayley ran to answer it. Christine Parker was at the door, holding a familiar-looking puppy carrier.

"Hi, everyone!" she said to Hayley and her family. "This is Daisy." Christine handed the German shepherd puppy over to Hayley.

Hayley stroked the puppy's soft fur and embraced her tightly.

Hayley's father looked at her. "Could I be your assistant?" he asked her.

Smiling, Hayley answered, "Sure you can, Dad."

Still holding the little shepherd puppy, she reached down to pet Koko. "I'd like to introduce Daisy," she told Koko. "Help us make her as good a Seeing Eye puppy as Pilot was."

Koko barked and wagged his tail.